Fern's Purple Birthday

Written by Claire Daniel

Illustrated by JoAnn Adinolfi

A Division of Harcourt Brace & Company

Fern Squirrel loved purple. She had thirteen purple shirts. She had thirteen purple skirts. Her purse was purple, and even her shoes were purple.

Fern's wallpaper was purple. Her bedspread was purple. Her sheets were purple, too. Even her stuffed horse had curly purple fur.

Fern loved PURPLE!

Fern's birthday was coming. On Thursday she was turning nine. "What do you want for your birthday?" asked Father Squirrel.

Fern didn't have to think long. "I want a purple cake. I want purple ice cream. I want purple gifts. I want purple snow outside! I want a purple birthday!"

"Oh, my!" said Mother Squirrel. "What can we do? I don't want to hurt Fern. How can we make everything purple?"

Mother and Father Squirrel went shopping. They bought a purple birthday cake. They found purple ice cream. Then they went to the pet store. They bought Fern a bird with purple feathers.

Mother and Father Squirrel still had a problem. It was going to snow. How could they ever make snow turn purple?

Mother and Father Squirrel turned down Third Street. They looked in a store window.

"I know what to do!" Father Squirrel said.

Father Squirrel told the store clerk what he wanted to purchase. "This is the perfect present for Fern!" said Mother Squirrel. "Can you wrap it in purple paper?"

It was Thursday. It was Fern's birthday. Would her birthday wish come true?

Fern looked up in the sky. It would snow soon. Would the snow be purple?

Fern's friends came to her birthday party.
They all had purple hats and purple horns.
They brought purple presents, too.

Purple balloons filled the house. Everyone ate purple birthday cake with purple ice cream.

Fern opened her first gift. It was from Mother and Father Squirrel. "It's purple sunglasses!" she said. "Thank you!" She put them on.

Fern looked at her friends. They were purple! She looked at her parents. They were purple! Fern looked at the snow. It was purple, too!

Fern Squirrel had a perfect purple birthday!